CAN YOU FIND MY LOVE?

Things With Wheels

JAN MARQUART

Copyright © 2015 Jan Marquart
All rights reserved.

www.CanYouFindMyLove.com

ISBN: 0967578094
ISBN-13: 9780967578095

Cover and Interior by Publish Pros
www.publishpros.com

Books currently available in the "Can You Find My Love?" Series

Seasons: Book 1
Things To Do Outside: Book 2
Why We Need Rain: Book 3
Things With Wheels: Book 4

Other Books by Jan Marquart

FOR ADULTS

Write to Heal
The Mindful Writer, Still the Mind, Free the Pen
The Basket Weaver, a Novel
Kate's Way, a Novel
Echoes from the Womb, a Book for Daughters
Voices from the Land
The Breath of Dawn, a Journey of Everyday Blessings
How to Write From Your Heart (booklet)
How to Write Your Own Memoir (booklet)
A Manual on How to Deal With a Bully in the Workplace
Cracked Open, a Book of Poems
A Writer's Wisdom

To:

paste
photo
here

_____
NAME

Thank you to all the parents, grandparents, teachers, doctors, daycare workers and others who have supported my efforts.

Also, my appreciation to Rich Carnahan, who continues to help me publish this book series and his son, Aiden, a special young man who has greatly influenced my work.

CAN YOU FIND MY LOVE?
was inspired by two little angels:
Landon James and Evelyn Kirsten.

Their proud parents are my sweet nephew, David Maravel, and his beautiful wife, Shawn Maravel.

You have received this book
because someone loves you.

Look closely—you will find love hidden
in everyday things that you might
normally take for granted.

This is what it looks like.

When you find the love I have placed
for you, I hope that it warms your
heart and lets you know how
very special you are.

Without wheels
objects could NOT roll.

Things with Wheels

CARS

Cars have five wheels—four on the ground and one inside to help turn left and right.

CAN YOU FIND MY LOVE?

DUMP TRUCKS

Dump trucks are used to move dirt and rocks from one place to another.

CAN YOU FIND MY LOVE?

School Buses

Big yellow school buses take kids to class where they learn new things.

TRAINS

The cars of a train are linked together and pulled along on rails by the engine.

MOTORBIKES

Motorbikes have rough wheels and go off-road where cars and trucks can't.

SCOOTERS

Push a scooter with your foot and roll away.

CAN YOU FIND MY LOVE?

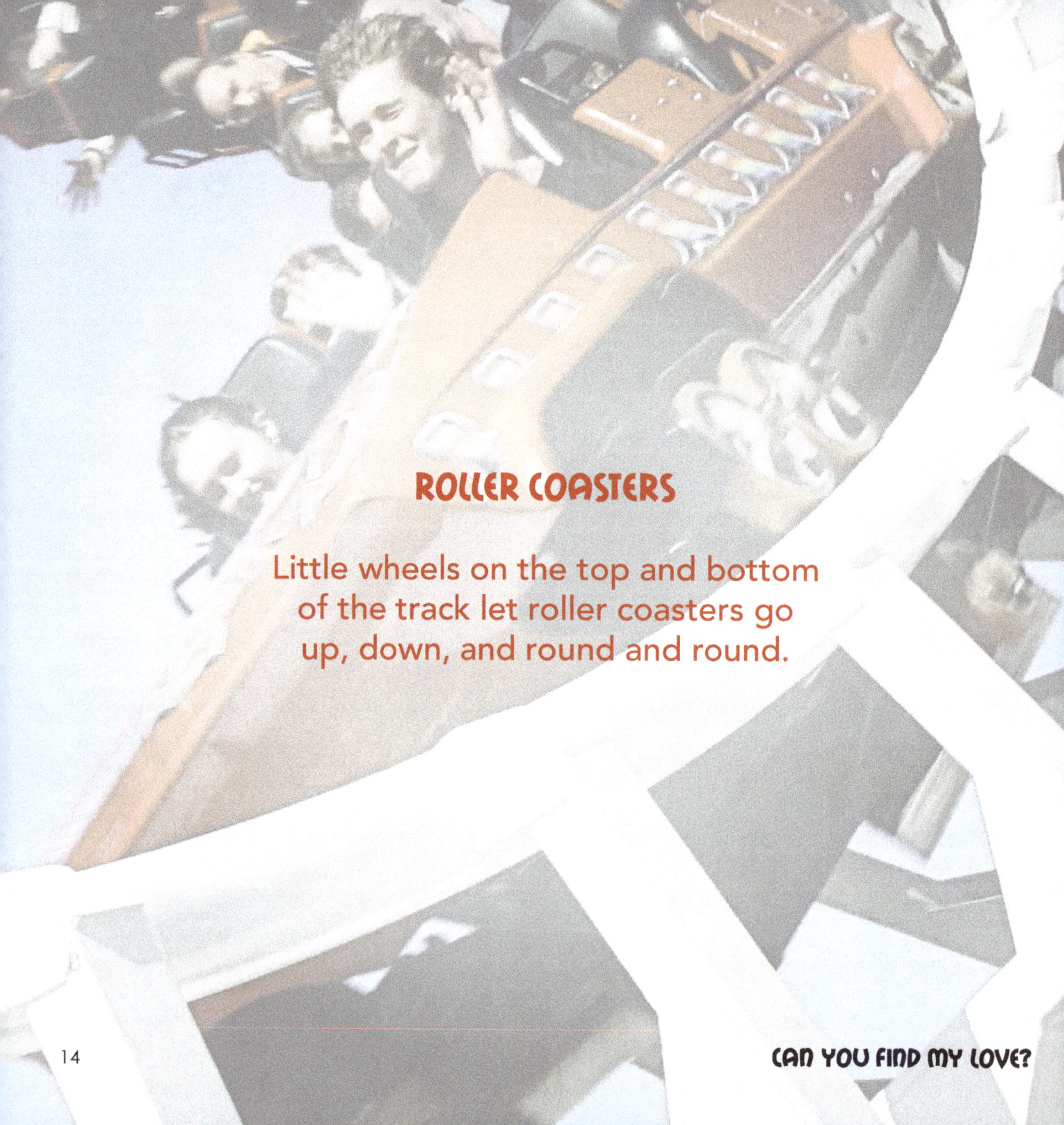

ROLLER COASTERS

Little wheels on the top and bottom of the track let roller coasters go up, down, and round and round.

AIRPLANES

Airplanes fly you around the world, but they can't land or take off without wheels.

CAN YOU FIND MY LOVE?

Wheelbarrows

Wheelbarrows help you carry heavy loads with ease using only one small front wheel.

MONSTER TRUCKS

The tires on these giant trucks are so big that just one can crush a car.

CARRIAGES

This fancy type of wagon was used before cars and is pulled by horses.

Rickshaws

Rickshaws are fancy bicycles that let passengers ride in a backseat.

GO-KARTS

Chase your friends in these miniature race cars that ride very low to the ground. Vroom! Vroom!

RECYCLE TRUCKS

Recycling is the process of turning used trash like cans, paper and bottles into new products.

TAXI CABS

When you can't use your own car,
taxi cabs take you anywhere in the city
you need to go.

CAN YOU FIND MY LOVE?

LAWNMOWERS

Lawnmowers are used to cut your grass to keep it short and healthy.

CAN YOU FIND MY LOVE?

TRACTORS

Tractors are used to help farmers plant seeds to grow crops.

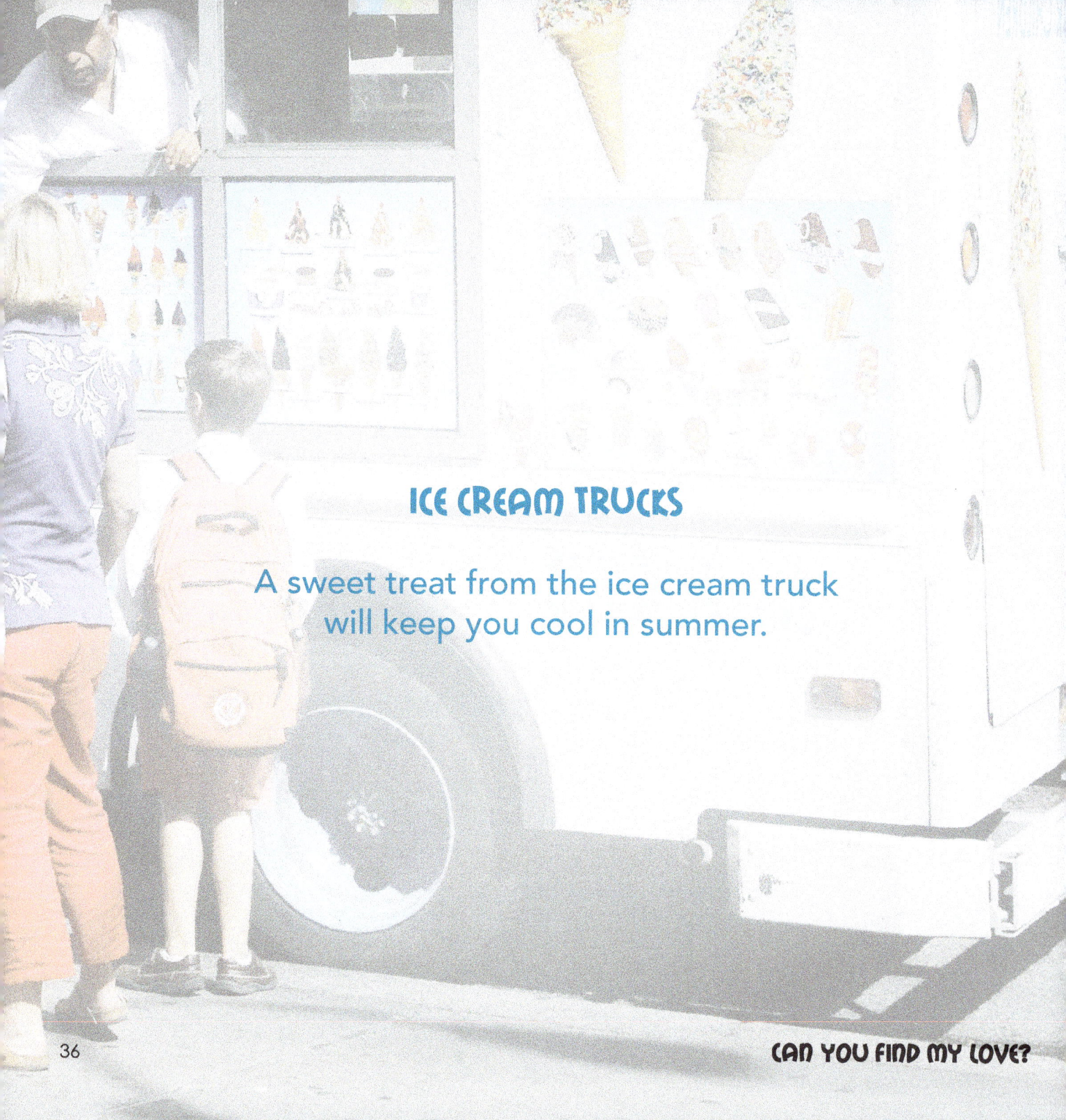

ICE CREAM TRUCKS

A sweet treat from the ice cream truck will keep you cool in summer.

Shopping Carts

These carts carry the things you plan to buy while you are shopping.

AMBULANCES

When you are sick or hurt, an ambulance takes you to the hospital.

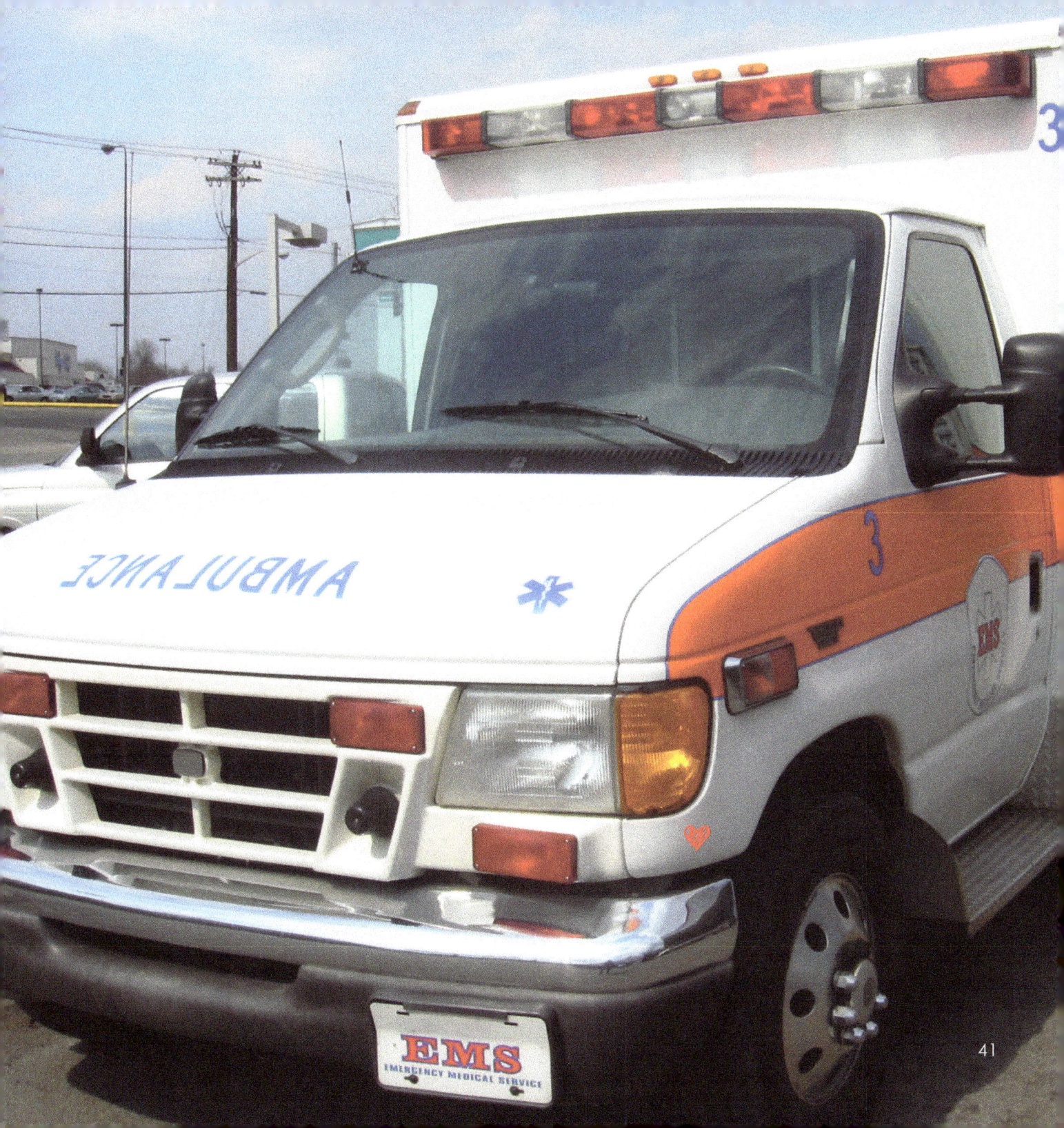

POLICE CARS

Police officers patrol the streets in these cars to keep you and your family safe.

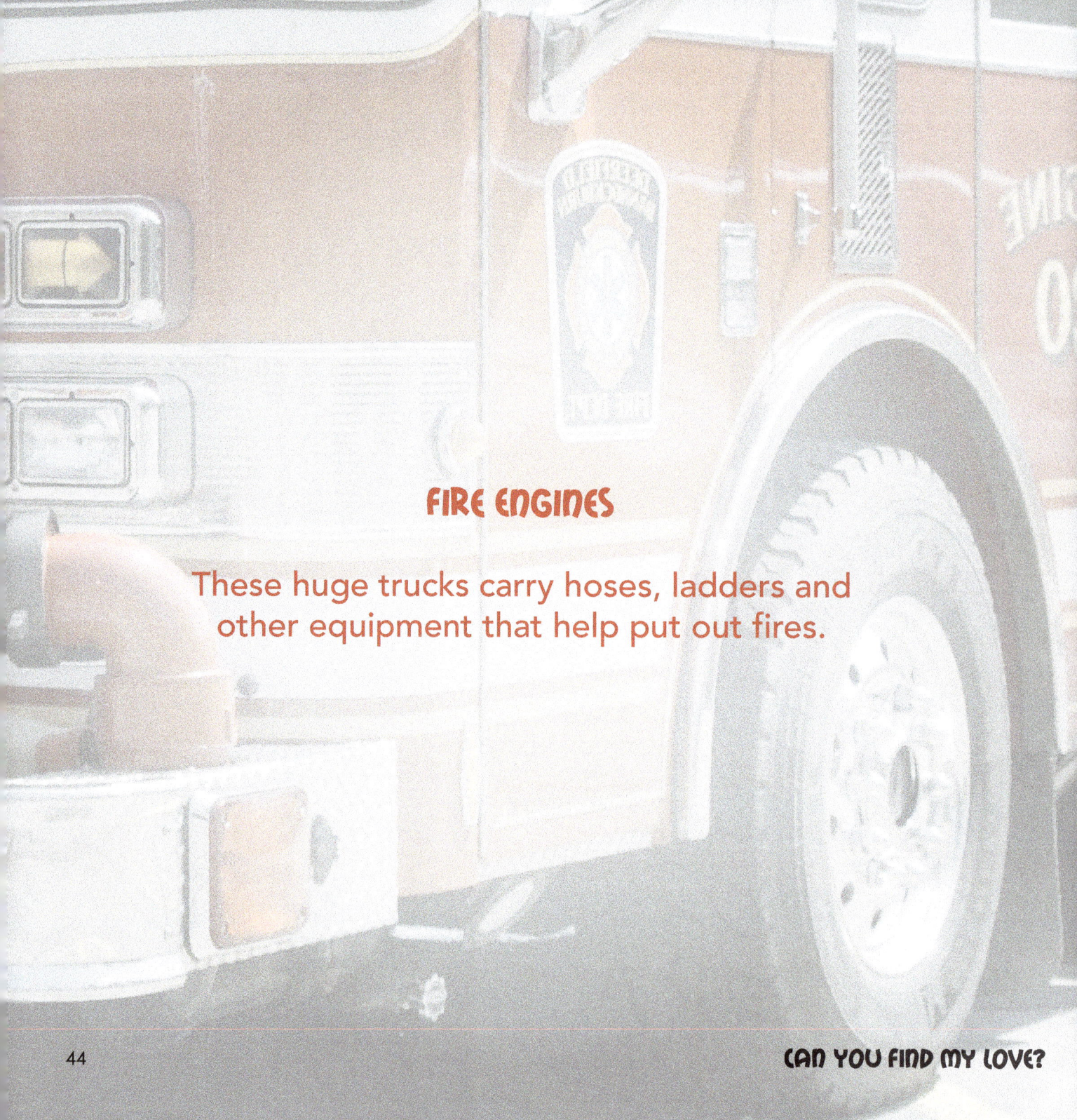

FIRE ENGINES

These huge trucks carry hoses, ladders and other equipment that help put out fires.

UNICYCLES

Unicycles have only one wheel and require great balance to ride.

CAN YOU FIND MY LOVE?

SKATEBOARDS

"Sidewalk surfing" strengthens your heart and tones your muscles.

ROLLER SKATES

Some roller skates have wheels in front and back and others have them in a row.

CAN YOU FIND MY LOVE?

BICYCLES

Some bicycles have extra wheels on the sides called "training wheels" that help you balance when learning to ride.

CAN YOU FIND MY LOVE?

Did you look close enough
to find all my love?

Can you **DRAW** a few other things that have **WHEELS**?

Can you **DRAW** a few other things that have **WHEELS**?

Can you **DRAW** a few other things that have **WHEELS**?

From:

paste
photo
here

_____
NAME

About the Author

Jan Marquart is a psychotherapist and author. She has published 11 books for adults and has had articles, stories, poems and essays published in various newspapers, journals and magazines across the United States, Australia and Europe. She teaches writing for those over fifty and has taught a dozen writing workshops for Story Circle Network.

Jan has designed a 6-week writing course titled *Unveil the Wounded Self - Write to Heal* which focuses on healing PTSD and has also designed a 6-week writing course titled *The Provocation of Journal Writing* to encourage everyone to write their personal stories. She is currently on her 99th daily journal.

Jan can be contacted at JanMarquart.com, JanMarquartlcsw.wordpress.com and at her personal email address, jan@canyoufindmylove.com.

Her books can be purchased from all major online book retailers.

www.ingramcontent.com/pod-product-compliance
Lightning Source LLC
Chambersburg PA
CBHW040247100426
42811CB00011B/1180